ROL
BANG!

ISBN #: 1880985-03-9
Fourth Printing
℗ ©**1990 Rollins / 2.13.61 Publications**

Layout and Design: Endless Graphics
Cover art: Peter Cunis
Back cover photo: Chris Haskett

BANG! is dedicated to Hatchman

Thanks: Stan, Gary I, Lynn, Peter, Don Bajema, Cubby Selby, Mitch Bury of Adams Mass

Soundtrack by: Tony Iommi, Geezer Butler, Bill Ward, Ozzy Osbourne

JOE COLE 4.10.61 - 12.19.91

2.13.61
P.O. BOX 1910 · LOS ANGELES ·
CALIFORNIA · 90078 · USA

2.13.61 Info line: (213)969-8043

Knife Street

Knife Street
Everything you want:
Cocksuckers, killers, diseases, love, war
People are geniuses here
They've found all kinds of ways to destroy you
They're also your friends
They want to fuck and kill you
Talking big and then shooting you full of holes
Full of Death
What the hell do you want?
Don't stick around here for too long or you'll get it
It all starts and ends here
All your dreams get raped here
The human will be overcome
The human will be destroyed
By other humans who couldn't handle their minds
Who couldn't handle their own balls
You're going to get it
In your mind
In your ass
In your veins
In your mail
In your soldier's hearts
It's hot
It's burning
It's real
Your mother raping your wounds
It's time for you to get the real feel of things
I want you to see what you have been doing in your nightmares
You got sold out
You thought that they liked you
They are scientists
Checking out their new drugs on you
And you like it
It takes you away and gives you back to them
You're always getting delivered
The ozone layer breaking doesn't scare the crack dealers one bit
More blood
More good times
More high roller games
It's all coming to a head

You're riding the big wave this time
You'll be right in time for this one
That's why you're going to get destroyed
You never learned restraint
Never had the guts
You'll learn mercy
It'll be encoded into your DNA
While you bleed and shit your pants
Here's a hole
Put your dick into it
Put your money into it
Like a circus ride
Get on the monkey's back and get taken for a ride
The garbage truck is coming
Throw yourself and your kin on board, you're going home
You made it straight and flat and now it's killing you
I'm laughing, it's not me
I don't exist, remember?
I didn't do the right dance
Never mind me, this is your party
I am the wall flower
Un-addicted
You know, I don't think you're tough
I think you're on drugs
I think you swallowed one of their super vitamins
And now you're running wild
I see you driving by, car stereo blasting thunder
Painted face cracking like a clown's
Shake hands with the 13 year old PCP dealer
Look at the black eyes
His father's eyes
The nights in the black room full of fear
Cutting his teeth
Learning a new and harsh language
Now he brings it to you
I see them, you
Lining up to be skinned
Seeing if they got what it takes
Getting their wings, getting them clipped
*We come from the suburbs to get destroyed. There's nothing
like it out there. We come here to see all the freaks and the*

violence. Hey who needs movies. Last week me and my friends
wasted a fag and we got his ears to prove it, you wanna see?
I got them right here. Wanna beer?
Knife Street always waiting
A mecca of understanding
Bleed on me, puke on me, it's all been done before. I don't care
if you live or die on me. I'm here for you, here to serve you. Here
to suck you right though your shoes. I got all the time in the
world.
So it speaks
The beast is always hungry
I can hear it at night,
Howling, telling me to get up and dance
To come into the fire
Get wet until the blood turns to dust
Re-hab to re-hab
Front door drugs, back door drugs
You can always score again
Junkies getting back into harness
After being free from the monkey for so long
So good to be back home
You're falling now, calling for help
They come running to give you more poison
Digging your grave deeper and deeper
The fourteen year old boy who sells you his dick
The burning bum
The long lines
You never get enough
Your stamina is amazing
Bullets, lots of bullets
Where do you go
Call the hot line
They're waiting to destroy you
The flowers explode
The cunning mind of a junkie
The art of lies
The blade that cuts so well
You bleed invisibly
The howling sun to take you away
Look into the eyes of the whore
Endless and burning

More truth than you can take
Run to the bar
It's time for more poison
Tie one on it's the weekend
They said that it's ok
Your shoes covered with vomit
Are wings to take you higher
You earned this
Open up, relax
The more you relax the less it'll hurt
This appointment is taking years
Do you ever wonder why you never get better?
The killers are lonely
They wrap the disease around you
They built the fire on the outskirts of town
Salvation vacation null and void salvation
The wind up and the pitch
Coming down from speed
She sees all the things for what they are
She never knew how ugly it all was
The drugs helped. They got her in touch with a lot of the bad
karma that she had been missing. She told me that it was a
lot better for her now that she had a handle on it all. She said
there was a lot of creeps out there.
*The more you do, the more you want to do. The more of these
people you meet, the more you like them. They become your
family, they take you in. They look after you, they sell you
things, they cut you deals. They help you with your habit.
Without them it's too hard to survive being hooked. I guess
when you get into it, you have to get into it all the way. It's my
life now.*
Slam monkey slam
Grinning bloody moon
Are you ready for the big one?
The super abortion?
Like a crack dealing uber insect
24 houraday mother comin' for ya
You're like that guy
That living dying god, Evil Knevil
Taking anything
A handful to get you on the trail

A handful to get you down it
High school life
Drug time, big time
A time of discovery
Like getting the shit kicked out of you for the first time
The first joint, Death's handshake
Welcome to the loser club
Sample goods from our duty free shop
It's your duty
It's part of growing up to be a good machine
Rock out on this trip
No one has ever taken this ride before
All those things that you heard, about how they took too much
Killed themselves
Turned into hallway legends, super freaks
Terminal subterranean minded
Slow boys and easy girls
That will never happen to you
They didn't know what they were doing
They didn't have the right stuff
Old wives tales
Like thinking that you can fly
Like forgetting how to breathe
Whoops, no sweat
A lie
You're the super thing
You'll never fall, you'll never die
The old wives rolling on the floor
Choking on blood and laughter
Fingering their scarred sex
Praying for you to get on with it
Join the club take a step down
It feels like up doesn't it
Fly like an eagle fuck head
You look sexy with a tag
on your John/Jane Dough toe
Slabbed at the city morgue
Chillin'
Boogie chillin'!
I can hear you revving your engines
The highways are yours tonight

Get the Andy Warhol action
Twisted accordion car, pedal to the metal
Let god put on the brakes
Attention thieves: The meat is here!
The veins are swollen
Come forward out of the darkness
Show them that they matter
Do what you do best
Go for that genetic imperative rock
Make'em into head lines
Get your paycheck and head for the hills
Castration starts in the womb
Pollution starts in the home
Let's make this a big year for disease
Let's take it over the top!
Always go to the source for your information
A lie is best when it's fresh
The bum in the pool of blood
Is scraped off the side walk and hauled away
The Mexican attendant
Hoses off the remains of the dead nameless
They are in love
They share everything
Nights of sex and sweat
Needles
Lies
A need to keep the monkey happy
The monkey wears a three piece suit
Works the high road
Keeps his blood clean
No monkey on the monkey's back
All for you
It's all coming your way
Like the fall preview that never stops
The smell of heart break comes running at your face
Spring makes you cry at night
Thinking of the way it used to be
The good times
Times that you know nothing about
You got it out of a book, out of a movie
A rose out of the Beast's mouth

The night rapes and confuses
We got the technology
No one gets out without getting a taste
Look at the survival rate
So far they are perfect
*We would like to thank you for making this the biggest year in
our career. Without you being so god damned helpful, there's
no chance we could have done it. Thanks to you, it works. We
take you and take you, and you keep on taking it and taking
it and we don't see how you can do it but you do it and we
thank you, god bless.*
This glorious violence
How long can you keep it up
I love the fury of the dying breed
It never gets as active as it does right before
The whole thing shuts down
I love the conviction of a loser
Only a loser has any
I love the lies of the well adjusted
It's not the truth, but an amazing substitute
It does the job
If it doesn't, you pay someone else to make it work
I love the music of your dying world
The sound of people crawling up their own asses
The children barely escaping
The destructive confusion of their parents
Learning crime as survival
Dodge the hand, duck the needle
Sidestep the drunk that gave birth to you
Monster to monster in your image
Hello new meat!
Alcohol's volcanic love bite
The youth scarred, sharpening their teeth
Getting ready to try
All the new things that you taught them
They always do it better
Up the ante
Make your parents proud
Letter from jail:
*Dear Mom and Dad: I made it. I'm in the roughest ward of the
whole prison. I have tried to kill myself three times, and all*

three times I've been stopped by this one guard. I'm working hard in shop class saving my money so I can buy him off and kill myself without hassle. I know I can do it.

Denial
It's always someone else with the problems
Some poor jerk
Never you
Stay away from those that kick the real jams
It's too real
You make me sick
It's ok
You'll taste the blood
It will be too late to do anything about it
You with your letters, your angry words
Can't you see that you aren't at war with me
You don't know me, don't give yourself that much credit
It's all yours now
You're the one that will have to be responsible
For all this blood
The saddest song ever written will be by a human
Probably some white dude
Talking about what's happening "right now"
I'm not always sure of myself
But I'm sure of you
I'm sure you will do all the things that you set out to do
Do it well
How much do they want
They want it all
Like the football coach said:
Make it hurt now so it won't hurt later
Never seems to stop hurting
Take care of it with the pain killer
The weekend approaching
Ready to spit blood fire gasoline
Obituary writers lick their lips in anticipation:
It's really hard for us obit guys, we do a lot of sitting around. It's not as bad as it used to be. In fact, it's getting better all the time. We love the holidays, it's a real call to arms for us. Don't take this the wrong way, but we all cheer in the office when the reports come in. "Die baby, die!" we always say. Not that we're into people dying, but hey, it does give us a chance to flex our

fingers if you know what I mean. So yeah, we like it when
someone gets smeared out all over the highway. But it's only
because we like to work, you know what I mean?
The bud trucks are starting their engines
The bars are oiling their taps
The whores are sharpening their blades
The pigs are cleaning their guns
Getting ready for the good times
FM radio barking out the commands
The religion
The love call for the Death trip riders
Rent a limo for that weekend concert night out. With all the
police on the road, you know you're going to get busted! So
party hard and leave the driving to someone else. Don't get
busted, ride in style!
Can you hear it?
In the street lights
In the stores
In the roar of midday downtown
Locking and loading, pumping up the insanity
Get busy
So many stories, all lies
No one really ever goes to jail
No one really ever gets raped
Do they
If it's not you, then who the hell cares
Some strange celebrity: Rape victim #2 million
Hello and welcome to rape rap, the call in show with a
difference. We take male and female callers who have never
been raped. That's right, never been raped! We hear their
questions, we give advice on how to prepare for the first one,
give advice to those who have never had intercourse before!
How to relax so penetration will be as painless as possible. At
rape rap, we say: Hey, let's get it out in the open so we can deal
with it. You're not alone on this, we're here to help we can even
arrange rape sessions! Tell you the hot locations to get raped,
how to dress to attract the rapist that you've been having those
nightmares about. Call in now!!
Do you ever look at your hands and see blood?
Good times
Punches in the stomach, all for you

By you, to you, from you
You scare me, I'm running
On top of the bar she is dancing, underage and unsure
The Beast is getting hungry
It's the same old thing
She's from the mid west, looking for something different
This will have to do for now
It won't always be this way
But for right now...
She can pay the Beast to let her live and drink the water
Good drugs in the water, helps you to sleep
Kill the pain
Kill the madness
Get on with the television show
The guy got wasted because he loved men
Another man killed him, it's a man's world
You ladies wouldn't understand
You just better get used to the stupid violence
Buckle up
It's a man's man's man's man's man's Knife Street
Get in the car and duck down
The killer intent of the boy hooker
The world's hardest hustling night act
A cure for every cure
We'll get you yet
Using the word nigger out loud, under the breath
Oh honey, you have nigger on your breath
Cars going by full of Mario Andretti killers
Masters of love call out
You would like to think that they are another breed
But you're the same kind
Me too
That's why I'm running scared away from the party
I'm thinking about tearing my face off
While I still have one
Baby born without finger prints
File it under missing person
So many of them
Shapeless remaining nameless
Boogie 'till you vote
No more poison, no more pain

That's not the way it goes around here
You want humanity?
You have to pay the price
Have you paid your dues?
Have you gone up on the cross yet?
The hard dirty blood of justified action
Fellas, it doesn't get any better than this
Fella with a beer in his hand
Fella with a gun in his mouth
Waiting on the god with the paycheck
All the time, they're trying to be angels
Seeing if they can fly
They get scraped off the ground by the other gods
The ones that didn't make it to the bank on time
Didn't make it to the morgue
Not you?
Oh yes you
Pay them to love you
Pay for the lie
Be nice to me, don't kill me
In the park, the man is working the crowd
A modern medicine man
Someone you can trust
At least he lets you know that he wants to kill you
The crowd erupts in applause
Another has been eaten by the Beast
*The war was something that we could never get too far away
from, we decided to make it our lives instead. You know how
it is, they tell you it's going to be one way and then when you
get there, whoa boy are you in for a surprise. That's it, that's
our lives, this war, this disease. You're never going to get out
of it, why don't you just get into it, I could show you some nifty
dance steps. Hey wait, don't go over there, those guys will
shoot you.*
Broken knuckle blues
Real love songs sung by the men with no real teeth
Lived by the ones with the old stare
The broken hands, the white noise television sets
Old wars screaming though the night
A lot of vomit, a lot of hard blood
The kind that comes out a bit at a time

Oh longo, long, long, longo. We come to hang our head in your dimly lit arena. Beer on tap it's always time to fade away, kill the dreams that we had, the dreams that we had. We came to our senses during happy hour. The men's room smells like Death, smells like home. Oh, oh, the blood runs like cheap wine on the well worn sidewalks of Knife Street. We have our myths. The man that went to jail for 1000 years, he drank here. Used to sit right where you're sitting now. Puked right over there, never cleaned it up, kind of memorial to the guy. The man that went and joined the Navy. Heard that he threw himself overboard. Well, we never saw his ass again. Longo, longo, long, long, longo. Long Beach you're our home.

Hanging on like bionic ticks
No lust for life, it's just love of disease
The ones that have become addicted to the disease
The survivors got smart and learned how to kill you
I can see it
Evolution happening right before my eyes
Babies born with broken knuckles
Already addicted to violence
It's good but it's going to get better
The hot nights on the roof
Sex and desperation
Thoughts of escape, pure fantasy
Don't let the master catch you thinking for yourself
There will be crime events in stadiums soon
Have a ghetto in Dodger Stadium
Turn two gangs loose in there
Give them what they want
Let them do what they do best
What they have been taught
Allow them to follow their genetic imperative
The crowd will go wild
The fans dressed in "colors"
Everybody who hates their lover raise their hand!
All of those who have been thinking about killing themselves
Testify!
At night I go out and listen to the Beast
I hear it sharpening its fangs
Eating whores, jacking speed
The Beast is out tonight filling them with hate and soul power

If I were you I would take it to the street
The ambulance drivers are like those pit stop teams
They haul you in so you can get rid of that pesky bullet
And get back into the game
Ok, you're all patched up, now get back out there and give 'em
hell. We don't want anyone to think that you're some kind of
slacker right? Right! You have a job to do like all the rest of us.
Hey, if it wasn't for you guys going out there and getting shot,
stabbed, slaughtered and mutilated, us guys would be like that
guy in the Maytag ad, right? You're hot, now here's some free
bullets. Get out of here, you're a maniac.
He drove your daughter all the way home in the trunk of his car
He shoved a coke bottle up your dad
He did a lot of things
There's no time to list them all here but you can go check it out
It's a pretty heavy duty achievement list
A man on a mission
A real work ethic happening here
A hall of fame for murderers
It's called channel 7
All the stars come out at night to suck and eat you
Get to the finish line
The dead line, the white line, the fine line
Think of what that is
What separates you from them
Television, money, a car
The color of your skin, the time you were born
Fences, green lawns, ignorance, apathy
Fear of: life, Death, bullets, work, confrontation
What you are, what you are becoming
Having to deal with yourself for the first time
Like kissing a new stranger
Not recognizing the breath
A destructive stranger coming to call
Coming to ruin your life
Knife Street passing though you like a train
On your hands and knees in the back of the limo
Choking on the poison
Villages burning
These sad tortured skies
This ugly heart

The black blood
Feel life's pain
A curse for you
Roll with it, swim though it
Disco abortion
It's alright if your name isn't signed to it
Do you have a lover?
Look into its eyes
Feel the pain
How many times have you lied today
Knife Street pushing though your chest
Light up another smoke
Finger your lucky number
Await the gas
Gas light
Arc light
How will you handle the final shove
The final love
The big joke fist
The big rock down your throat
The bitter taste
Overwhelming
Do you feel it rising?
Oh baby I can feel it, give it to me
I don't care who's looking
I don't care what happens
Sex like a suicide pact
The last lie will be the best
That's the way to do it
Save the best for last
And then you fall diseased and breathless
Cold and friendless, sullen and endless
Distorted and selfless, broken beyond repair
A bad machine with bad habits
Make your eyes look backwards though your mind
Try to find the face
The first face of the million that took you
Took you for everything
Try to remember the place where the first violation occurred
Was it a good time?
Did you get your money's worth?

Do you feel the rope around your neck?
Do you see the man on the corner?
Smiling and holding his hand out?
Is it real or is it you?
Is that a window or is that a mirror?
Is that a limousine or a hearse?
Did you win lose or draw?
Are you fearless yet?
Have you seen enough to where you can't see anymore?
Can you laugh at everything yet?
Our ancestors had bigger tear ducts,
But smaller brains
Locked in tight, making love to the machine
Modern gods:
Smith and Wesson
Jack Daniels
They help you see who you are
How much you can take and how low you can go
In the dead of the night
I can hear every alarm in the world
Ringing
Buzzing
Screaming:
Don't get destroyed
Don't get taken
Don't get choked on your emotions
Get your arm out of the machine
Get the monkey off your back
No one listens to alarms
The sound, so loud, so clear
Goes unnoticed
Pathetic addict
Hand in the machine
Somewhere, there's got to be a prayer for you
Somewhere, a bullet's flying,
Looking for a home
A roach is giving birth
Thank god all is not lost
There's still something they can take
Your soul's not enough
Your mind was too easy

Are you into this or not?
Stop hiding
Give it up
You're blocking
Watch out, you might get busted for resisting unrest
Last week she got visited by a man with two heads
His blood rushed to both and he did what there was to do
She's a comedian of sorts now
She doesn't talk
But she sure walks funny
You're getting pushed
Shoved
Smile and love it
It's all on file
And soon we'll all know the truth about you
What little there is of it left
You're like us
A million pairs of hands reach out to you from the subway
Calling to you:
Get up
Get into it
Get involved
Shake the man's hand boy
Shake your father's dick boy
Shake your past
Shake the recurring reality
Shake the rage
Hey!
Cool it man you're shaking
The boy goes rock climbing
Says he's up, high as a kite
But he's always down on the corner
Soon the new blues:
*Born in the Holland Tunnel, came to the city through that
insidious funnel. Looking for fortune, fame, good times and
dames. Went into business minding other people's business.
Needed that edge. Found that money doesn't have to sit in
savings. That razors are for more than just shaving. Chopping
lines isn't making an edit. You don't have to be for real if you
have credit. He got ugly, fat, stupid and desperate. They made
a movie about him, called it "Just Another Sucker". I know it's*

true it's me. I'm a half way man.
Both eyes open, one eye blind
Turned the other cheek so many times
He broke his neck and died
Pity
Could've gotten a few more years out of him
Do you ever hear the drums, the call of the warriors?
Do you ever feel like you're walking though someone else's movie?
Like you don't belong?
It's ok, you belong
You're locked in tight
The first time you get out will be the only time
And the drag is, you'll know what hit you
You'll have 200 shares of it
Just understand this:
You were never one of the beautiful people
Sweep away the ash
Separate the cinder from the bone and teeth
Separate the humanity from the scum
Understand the impossibility of separating something from itself
That whore staking out that corner
Hands on hips, wide stance
Hungry
New food for the new flesh
War stories fill the air
Find the jungle in the city
Soon everywhere will be the bad part of town
Coffee, tea or a shot
This time it comes down hard
In brutal, choking, easy to read
User friendly language
Beautiful, terminal, action
It's gonna be a party y'all
Like Do Long bridge
You learn from criminals
Too chicken hearted to identify yourselves
To choose what side you're on
You choose it or it chooses you
Hunts you down, lines you up
You know, there's no place like home
With all the things that will get done

To you
By you
You might as well say good bye to the home front
Take a spin though the old streets
Take a friend
Show your friend where you got raped
Show your friend where you saw that man get shot
Don't show your friend where you used to jump and play
Don't let anyone know you ever did anything like that
They will hold it against you
Use it against you
All the things that happened don't count
Remember your mother's embrace
Things are breaking down
They're lying at your feet
Get your galoshes out
Don't get any on you
This game will not tilt
This fire only stops when there's nothing left to burn
What a beautiful inferno
A siren song
Knife Street dying
The big cleansing
Iron sanity
From the ruins, a bigger, better one will be built
We know ourselves very well now
Fire up the engine
Put another child on the grill
Get psyched, get ready, get set
The Beast is screaming
Filling your ears
Telling you to come forward
There's no place to hide on Knife Street

American Hardcore

Checkout at the market. There she is. Baby in one arm, five year old at her feet. The purchase: six of bud, fifth of Old Granddad, pack of Kools, potato chips (bar-b-que), tampons. The cashier checks the bruises on her arms, rings it all up. She's short, she puts the tampons back. Priority.

Yelling cursing noise level terror. Then he hits her. She cries, things get quiet then it starts again. Locked in his room, the boy sits on the floor next to his bed. That's the place he goes when they go at it. Mother and Alien, this man/boyfriend. This thing that watches television and drinks long cans of malt liquor in the dark. Sometimes the Alien is there when his mother isn't. The Alien doesn't talk. The Alien drinks, beats mother and watches television. The boy knows that he's lucky the Alien doesn't beat on him. Aliens beat on his friends. He sees them at school with their bruises. He figures that Aliens are here to make life hard as possible.

He steals his father's pot and sells it at school for beer money. Gets drunk when ever possible, fucks shit up. Cuts classes, comes into third period high. Steals shit from stores at the local mall. Wrecked his friend's father's car. Listens to FM radio, watches television. Seen a video of his father screwing some young blonde chick that he wouldn't mind doing the same thing to. Knows the alarm codes to all his friend's houses. Plans to be in a rock band some day. Has ripped off a guitar in preparation for this.

I'm going to punch you into next week. I'm going to punch you so hard that you'll have to pull down your pants to brush your teeth. I'm going to clean your clock. I'm going to kick your ass. I'm going to start World War III on your face. Take off your glasses, this is going to hurt. Take the first motherfucker. Don't start with me. It's been about 5 minutes since I kicked the dog shit out of a butt face faggot motherfucker like you. If you see a faggot then I think you better slap him. Let's take it outside. I'll meet you here after class, after the show. I'll see you in the pit. Watch your back. See you around motherfucker.

Afterburn

Rhythm of decline
Do the choke dance
All night long
Get it right
You find yourself in the land of the lost
You fit in
Disappear into the background the soundtrack blaring
Relaxing in the ghetto
Picking the glass and plaster out of your hair
Some party, everything smells dead
Perversion
Distortion
Decadence
Low tide going lower

What happened to your body
You used to be so good looking
It looks like a storm ripped though your eyes
Looks like you were rung out
Pasty dry skin
Sagging, paint peeling
What?
No shit
Crystal meth?
That shit tore you up
You look like you've been fucked,
By the Army, the Navy
And the Lower East Side
Damn girl, you used to be so fine

I see you walking though the ruins
Broken child lost
Blown apart and schizophrenic
Where are they now, your friends I mean
Let's sit down here and watch the sun set
Yes, you're right, there used to be palm trees over there
Yes, they were destroyed
What's that smell?
That's napalm son

Nothing else in the world smells like that
Here's a word for you son,
Can you say "ghetto"
Good, all you have to do to keep away the evil spirits
Is to say it to yourself,
Every time you inhale

———

I used to love you
I still do
So selfish
I love the old you
The you that doesn't shoot drugs
The you that didn't get beat on by men
You laugh in my face and call me a fool
But it's true
I still love you
Sometimes, I can see the old you
When your eyes flash
When you look
Almost
Alive

———

He sits in the folding chair
He stares at his hands
All the scars
Fist to face
Fist though glass
Fist though wall
Where to now
Glory is an echo
He listens to the others tell their stories
They all sound the same
He thinks to himself:
Re-hab isn't a road, it's a treadwheel
He looks at the men he's sharing the wagon with
Faces hollow
Seen ghosts
Seen Vietnam
Seen Korea
Seen Beverly hills
Seen too much too many times

They sit in a circle confessing
Coming clean
Wagon wheel
Lonely, holding on
Still addicted to addiction
The florescent lights make them look injured
Soon, time to go home
And wait until next week to get back together
And sing the old songs

———

Awoken from a dream
He looks out the window
Three a.m.
What happened to the last two years?

———

Running away
Curling up
Hiding
No use
Just abuse
He conceals his pain and horror
Life could be so great
Without them

———

He got raped by his mother's boyfriend
You think I'm joking
I wish
I was

———

The disease
Died broken hearted
There was no one left
To infect

———

A long time from now
There will still be someone telling you
How great it all was

———

There was a time
When things weren't so...
And the air was...

And people were...
When you could go about at night
And not hear
Gunshots

———

27 to life staring him in his face
Hanging out with him in his cell
Following him to the shower
Putting him to bed at night
He's got a lot of brothers
Friends as a gesture
On the edge of violence
The thing that keeps everyone together
He doesn't want to be a faggot
It's hard
No woman in 7 years
What the hell was it like?
How did it feel?
There they are
The walls
There it is
The time
There it goes
Life passing

———

"My Dead Friend"
(Sung to the tune of Three Blind Mice)
My dead friend
My dead friend
See how he lives
See how he lies
He got himself to the halfway house
He's half way there and he'll never get out
You should hear the trash
That comes out of his mouth
My dead friend

———

She was raped by her uncle
Her father left home for another man
She is confused
She is sixteen

———

He never told anyone about the beatings
The time his father broke his arm
He yelled so loud
That the neighbors called the police
Now he lives with strangers
They're alright
He's had the closet door taken off its hinges
He doesn't let anyone touch him

———

York Pennsylvania
Six confirmed kills
Walked point
Talks about his buddies
Some are too freaked out to come out of their houses

———

Listen!
Hark!
Machine gun music in the sky
Police chopper
Electric warrior
Round up from above
Random gunshots somewhere in the palm trees
I sit in my hole
Safety in #1
At night LA glitters like a woman
That got punched in the mouth
And got told to get her ho ass back to work
Listen!
Hark!
I think I hear an angel!
Oh
It was just a pig

———

What was that shit they all said to you? I forget, you told me
the last time. Yea, that's right, they said that you were going
to turn into a robot if you kept smoking that shit. What was
it again? Oh yea, that's wild, cigarettes dipped in lysol. Man
I bet you could hear the brain cells cooking. What was it
like? What, you don't remember? Do you ever have dreams?
What do you think about? Man, you're scorched. No wonder
they call you "Terminal."

———

How many years on the job?
How many kids at home?
What's her name?
No, your wife's name
What is life?
How many drinks after work?
Where did your life go?

I'm lost. I don't understand. There are a few things that I can remember. I have dreams of him touching me, dreams of his tongue. I swore to myself that if anyone ever touched me like that again I would kill them. The dreams never stop. I am afraid he'll be there to rape me again. I know I do it to myself. Why do I do this. Do I hate myself? I rape myself in my dreams. I torture myself daily. I murder myself at night. I let him into my dreams. I've tried to have boyfriends. I don't want to be alone. I like boys, it's hard to deal with it when they want to touch me. I know that there's nothing wrong with what they want to do but I can't do it. They call me bitch, castrator, tease. They don't understand. I am so scared and alone. I wish someone would hold me. I'm so cold, why doesn't anyone understand? I can't talk to anyone. Sometimes I want to die. I feel that I will go though life with no one to love me. The only one who ever told me that he loved me was him. Maybe that's why I keep having the dreams. Please god let there be someone to love me besides him. Someone on the planet to love me. I see the looks on people's faces. The world is cold and mean. People are wild and dangerous. Someone to love me. Please don't let me go though life like this.

I miss you. I know that I keep saying that and I know that you're getting tired of me writing you all the time but I can't get over the fact that you're gone. I know that you only live across town but I tell you it's hard driving by that house you share with that guy and knowing that all the time he's using you. You know that he's using you don't you? You never did listen to me. I have some friends that hang out in this club that he goes to. I'm told that he hands you some pretty heavy beatings. I hear that he's selling you on the street. I'm afraid to go over there and knock on the door and talk to you. I'm

---

afraid he might kill me. Are you using drugs? You never needed to when you were with me. Can I see you again? Will you call me? Will you at least call me? I miss you.

———

Kicking it live with a human wreck
Do you see the one
That stares you in the eyes when you look in the mirror?
Who the hell is that?
I know
I never seen him before either

———

Turned subterranean ruthless a new education humans stuffed living museum pieces turned inside-inside inbred wrong shoes on wrong feet stumbling into work lying to keep it together. After a while the pain goes away. What sets in? Earner of the new scars, the new promotion, the new flesh sold by the pound, worthless breathless. What happened to romance? Someone raped it, turned it into a movie, turned into never-never land. Always waiting for the crash, the earthquake, the break in, the drive-by shooting, the football game. Waiting to see if the man caught on. Hurry, sneak in a quick beating while the machine isn't looking. Get some action before the shift starts, before it's too late, before they come home, before the sale ends. It's all final. You can stay alive a little longer if you have credit. Put your blood in a washing machine, it's dirty. Kill the man that's breathing your air. Be the first, be the last to leave. Survival is like a video game, love is like the lottery, pain is like the boss, truth is like the wife, fun is like the pot of drugs at the end of the hall. The reward is yet to come. It's in the end zone, the full color wine cooler ad come to life. The spotlight is a very small circle. Who are you letting into your circle. Who's the enemy, who's the lover? Drink your fill, get your kicks before it decides that it causes cancer. The next world war will start across the street.

Blues Jam in the 213 Area Code

Everybody is somebody else's freak
Think about it
Sit at home with the television on
Watch some people burn shit down thousands of miles away
Look at those freaks, they're something. Must be rough over there
Outside, a killer is checking you out
Thinking to himself about the freak
Propped up in front of the television set
That's you
Everybody is somebody else's joke
You laugh all the time
You're always up for a laugh
Point your finger and laugh
Put it all below you
Meanwhile
The monkeys are laughing at you from their cages
From their glass boxes
You laugh back and throw excrement
You go back and forth and laugh and throw
But it gets to you
You wonder what's so funny
What's the matter
Can't take a joke?
Tag, you're it
He's laughing his ass off
You do look funny with the gun at the side of your head
And his cock in your mouth
Who's the freak now?
You're one of those bad trips
One of those things you read about
Don't bite
You might get shot in the head
Hey
I don't know if you get what you deserve
All I know is that you get it
Sleepwalker with the "boob job"
Yea get one of those
You'll need it
Otherwise fuckhead won't fall in love with you

When he grabs the top of your head and tells you to get busy
Just think of it as an investment
Get yourself well-oiled for the life-long sell out
Drive down the Blvd
Look at the young boy working the corner
Waiting for my father to pull up
Look and laugh right?
That's not you
You couldn't touch a reality that fierce to save your life
Look at the freak
Don't look for too long
Or he'll rip that smile right off your face and hand it to you
And then he'll start laughing
You're a ripe apple on a low branch
You're a filet in a shark tank
You were born human
Perfect for gang rape, mutilation, prostitution and glory
Everybody is somebody else's excuse
Perfect
All you need to get by
A point man
So you can have a reason to point a finger
To be able to escape yourself one more time
That wasn't me, I was drunk
You know how it is
That's not my fault, I was in love at the time
The pressure of the city made me do it
I took drugs to get away from my father
I drank to get away from my boss
I go to the bar to loosen up from the hassle at work
I hit my wife
Because the car wouldn't start
Because our son won't listen to me
It's not me with the problem
Someone else will take care of my sins
Some medicine will be invented
Someone on television will say something
And everything will be alright
And since I can stop any time I want to
Don't tell me how to run my life
I'm free

I heard that in a song on the radio
The cesspool of love
Festering swamp
Hear the blues song
The one about the man sitting alone in his room
Waiting
Hoping that maybe she will come back
It's all because of her
All this pain
All this sweat
Heavy thoughts
Like:
I don't want to live
I can't live
There is no sunshine
There is no life
There is nothing without her
So when that woman comes staggering back in
There will be a hot fist of love waiting
It's nothing but the blues
Keep your blues to yourself
Unless you want every pore, every hair,
Every thought you possess
Bought and sold at the speed of light
Blood, dust and an empty six
Spent shell casings, a broken television
A bent spoon, dirty sheets
Broken glass, the smell of rotting beer
Stale sweat, dreams of nowhere
You want mercy?
A break from the plague?
Arms to hold you?
A kind word?
Then get out of the 213 area code
It's all the blues around here

Death Song

I stand at my window and listen
I hear the sirens
One after another as they wail by
Sirens, gunshots and helicopters
All the time in this neighborhood
I'm lucky
I live in a good one
The Beast has been wounded
It crashes though the underbrush, roaring and snorting
The Beast is so heavy, and has been running for so long
That it will take years for it to fall
Meanwhile we wait in all kinds of spaces
Watching television, marveling at the criminals
The ones with the most charisma are the ones that we root for
Glad it's not us
The Beast is howling tonight
Trying to pull the shrapnel from its joints
It's coming to blood and rust
Blood and rust
That's all that will be found of me
When they come to see why I didn't pay the rent
They'll say: Yea, he was part animal, part machine
But that wasn't enough
Tell what's her name to get in here and clean this up
To make it though the Death song
The right stone throw
The right dance through the mine field
It's all in the walk and how you stand up
To intimidation, humiliation and violence
The beast is shuddering at my blues song
Showing its teeth
1000 suicide glory thoughts later and I am still here
It's still here
The cars are crashing tonight
Blood and rust
The last few nights
There have been gunshots across the street
The fact that the police never come
Doesn't mean a damn thing

You see what I mean?
Last week I was in the midwest
Omaha, Nebraska
There was real rain, heat lightning
The sky was swelling
Electric snakes coiled and struck
Darting in and out of warrior clouds
They looked like they were going to explode
I asked him if this would be a good place to move to
He said no, nothing ever happens here
It's a hollow faceless song that this place leaves you singing
All alone to yourself
As you clap spoons on the kitchen sink
To keep time with the crime
Hey, that rhymes
As crime goes by...
As I sit in a doorway thinking
This girl told me that she wanted to join the circus
A real circus
I asked her since when is the one
On Hollywood Blvd not good enough?
She didn't think I was funny at all

Black Sabbath

So much litter out of place
It's time to put it in its place
A mind is a terrible thing
A dream is flashing
Like a polished weapon in my mind
To the summer ambulance
Siren songs
The two drunk girls
Fighting outside the club
Broken glass under the crime lights
Fuck these streets and the bastards that put them here
All these experiments
Like how much blood will it take to drown you
All the while I know
That I am a hero in the making

A walking legend
Superstar status is my domain
If I had a car big enough,
I would drive all of you right off the edge
But there is not the time to play games
I walk the streets
Looking at you, listening to you
Living your garbage cowboy coward fantasy
This place is going to look a lot different
After I get done decorating
Too bad you won't be here to see it
I am an angel
I am a soldier
I am on a mission
No one knows but me
The streets talk to me
The sidewalk looks up at me and makes faces
It mocks me
When I breathe in, the stench fills me
Tries to consume me tries to destroy me
It will not destroy me
I am here to clear the air
Look at this place
Look at the filth, look at the decadence
It forces you to pick a side
Either you destroy it or you become it
Every moment of the day it stares you in the face
Taunting you, destroying you
And you let it
Tag
You're it
You're shit
It's too late for "spiritual awakening"
Fuck that hippy shit
It's too late for "social change"
You can't educate a flock of sheep
Can't you see that's what they want?
They want you to turn away
They want you to lie down
Like a lamb for the slaughter
Like a chump for the sellout

There will be no revolution
There will be no uprising
There will be no race war
How could anyone be that stupid
How could anyone believe that bullshit
What a joke
I know a lot about jokes
I see them all the time
I spent years with some living jokes
You should see them now
Fat stoned cowards
Living Death
Men of action turned into weak pieces of shit
They could get my respect again
If they shot themselves in the head
At night I walk the streets
I take mental notes
I take inventory
The filth, the garbage, the stench rising
Liars, freaks, clowns
My mission becomes clear to me
My life focuses into a laser beam
My purpose
Incinerate
My vision is pure napalm
I am here to clean
There's only one way to clean
You have to incinerate
You must cleanse with fire
You must turn disease to ash or it still lives
Things have gone too far
The strong are destroyed by the weak
Decadence has set a precedent
It's become a way of life
Not the way of my life
Shit is shit
I'm here to burn it
Can't you see
I'm beyond your shitty little world
I don't believe in equality
That is to say

That I don't think that if you're alive
That's all you need to get by
The man who sells drugs is not equal to me
The man who rapes his son is not equal to me
They cannot hide from me
Guilt trips will not shield them from me
I don't believe in human rights
I think you have grown fat and evil
Hiding behind your human rights
Reveling in filth
The balance must be brought back
When I walk the streets in my neighborhood
Faggots blow kisses to me
Drunks come staggering from bars
Guns go off
Police helicopters fly above
Yet nothing happens
Some show
Let's cut the drama
Get rid of the display
The ritual is nowhere
It's hollow
The nights are made of tin
Cheap, bitter Death
I'll show you my world
I'll bring it home
My beauty
The summer nights of fire and truth
Can you see it
A dark hot night
The whine of engines from above
The tree line explodes in fire orange
The air fills with the smell of gasoline
The air strike
Like a flower erupting in rapid birth
Filth turned to ash
So beautiful
Decadence lies bleeding
As I walk and plan
I hear angels singing Black Sabbath songs
The soles of my shoes are thick

Keeps the blood and urine at a distance
The mind I occupy is iron
My time is now
I see them
Maybe it's you that I see
Singing the song of the loser
Your endless diseased song
The end is coming
And I'm the one who's bringing it
I am the punchline
I will defoliate before it's too late
You spend millions on rehabilitation
Re-washing the brainwashed
Trying to come off
Like criminals were something you didn't make
There's no such thing as rehabilitation
How big does a lie have to get
Before even you can no longer avoid it
You shit in your bed
You wait for someone to come and clean it up
Well, here I am
Ready to throw out the baby with the bath water

War Pigs

Terrified
You
Sucking the television set
Wishing reality was video
Humiliated
Raped
On the lookout
Pick a side
See the man
Equipped with the zero remorse factor
And the anti-personnel device
That's a gun that kills you
Look at your friend feeling up your wife
Don't just stand there, do something
Call the pigs, they'll help

You better get busy, everybody has a war
Where are you at?
You're not going to sit this one out
You have to get hot
Look hard, find someone to hate
Better yet, don't hate anyone
Just kill them for the hell of it
Like that last hit of ex you took
Flash the peace sign
Go to one of those marches
Pick up a sign
Yell some shit about saving some animals
Then go home
Lock and load war pig
You never know when you'll have to get real

Lord of This World

Look at the gun
Fortune teller
No fiction, the best truth you will ever get
Loaded and walking cold
Looking for a friend
Searching for love on these mean streets
Look at the gun you dumb fuck
Like a pig sweating you
Do you have one yet?
Make the gun dance
Learn the language
Dance the new slow dance
Better than a computer game
I can see it now
You on the ground
The smell of your shit
The sound of the sirens
Talked tough to the wrong guy
Trying to look good to your date
He laughed and cold smoked your ass
He speaks the language
He knows the new dance steps

Make the gun prick up its ears
Pray and be prey
Or get loaded
Lord of this world
Riding the bus
Talking sweet to the ladies
Looking at you and smiling
Knowing full well bullets don't care
Choke
Look out your window
History is being jacked

Electric Funeral

Alone in the room
Over did it
Ended up a blues song
Everybody loves you now
They all want to say that they knew you
Lucky women got to know the real you
Don't worry
None of them will ever say anything
About how you were too high to fuck
The moron on the rock television
Telling you he's sorry for being a killer
He's all better now
Don't worry, he's still wild
But not as wild as he used to be
Look at the Hollywood bitch
Face sagging to her tits
She used to look like something human
Three of her ex's died this year
Pounded into the soil by the needle
They had a party for him
Played his records at some club
Told stories about how wild he was
He's not so wild now
Another electric funeral
Take that one for the road and sell it
Make a t-shirt

Put on a hard face
Talk like you've seen some shit
What a joke

Tomorrow's Dream

No more streets
No more cities
Paths line the forests and plains between villages
People laugh
They tell stories to the young ones
About how the old ways fell in on themselves
How the streets burned
Melted into the sewers, and disappeared
How the ugly ones took too much, too fast
How they choked on humanity and illusion
And went the way of the weak
At night while the city stabs and pimps,
Some watch and wait
Keeping themselves sane and clear
With tomorrow's dream

Tiny Master

You rock and rollers
Cowards
Harnessed, castrated
Tame, timid, weak
The craziest thing you can do is overdose
Useless disease spreaders
De-fanged, de-clawed
There ought to be a law
I see you prancing about
Your entire thrust a commercial
You freaky stepping stones
MTV
You took it to heart
You're taking the whole trip down the drain
Neutralized

Swimming in a sea of used bath water
That's what your music's like
Luke warm
You cowards
How could you do it?
How could you approach the Beast
And not be a warrior
I don't care what you think you are
Or what your managers and cocksuckers tell you
We both know what you are
You're going to cry when you hit thirty
Those tattoos turning blue
Your hair dye running
The lines in your face
The pose slipping
How you'll clutch
All of a sudden you'll see that you blew it
You fell for it
You'll get sold out so hardcore
That not even your re hab counselor will be able to help you
And to all of the suckers that you took with you
I don't give a fuck for a sucker
A nation of suckers
A world of suckers
Your people
I am the war that you will not win
I am the hard sell
Money doesn't do a motherfucking thing to me
Word

Goldenboy

How do you like the new golden boy?
Magic parasite on the corner
Made to order
Soon to die
Sucking sucking sucking
1-2-3-4
Criminal arise
Lick the ashes from the wounds

Lick the blood from the mouths
Smack your lips
Pack your piece, hit the streets
Real rock and roll
Get up early
There's a lot of new flesh to mutilate
The fields of bodies
Lost, selfless, slaughtered daily
You can do so much when you're stupid
When you trust
When you open wide and say
I do
Back to the golden parasite
Love affair with millions
Blood letting in the home
Amazing what you can do when you put your mind to it
Terrifying what you will do when you can't control it
Day after day
Paying sick homage to the god
The golden parasite
Walking on coals, doing 1001 dances
Expending
Fighting off the urge to end it all
Didn't you know it's already over?
That's how it goes with the parasite
The golden sucker
The sexy mind fuck
Death's cheerleader, that's our boy
I keep waiting for you to drop
I keep thinking that I'm going to read about you
And how you fell
But it never happens
I don't know where it all came from
I want to tell you about a man
A real man
I watched him sweat, bleed and scream
Through hot lit nights of brutal human tests
Sometimes I thought he was going to explode
Or burst into flame
He scared me, inspired me
Pushed me upwards and onwards

Like there's any other way to go
I watched him die
I saw it happen right in front of me
He gave up
Curled up and stepped off the line
Now he sits behind a desk
Stoned, overweight, paranoid, evil
All the things that he sought to destroy
He became background music
The golden parasite shakes his fist in triumph
And racks up another one
I think of him sometimes
Wondering when he'll pull down
One last shot at reality
Goodbye, goodbye
Sweep your ashes out the door
Yea kill yourself, but not here
Ok, well do it here
But could you wait for a commercial break?
The golden parasite gleaming in the sun
Hell yes turn it up
But don't get out of line
Come on in and get destroyed
That wise ass kid
Six months in the womb
Somehow the little bastard got a fax machine in there
Worked out a three movie deal
Sued his parents
Complained about the food
Said that the PCP she was doing gave him headaches
Things are different now
The water tastes funny
Easier to get a bullet than a good cup of coffee
Soon the whole thing
Will be up your ass

1000 WAYS TO DIE

#1
She broke
Her soul
On his feelings
Simple

#2
She
Played him
Like a
Knife

#3
When she
Vomits
I go
Wild

#4
She doesn't
Love me
She doesn't
Love herself

#5
When
Touches me
Parts of me
Ignite

#6
Breaks like
Glass
Cuts like
Love

#7
Girls
Like her
Make guys
Like him

#8
Stop
Wrecking yourself
On
My time

#9
Kill yourself
But
Not
Here

#10
When she
Calls my name
I know she
Doesn't know me

#11 To
      Realize
      One's
      Will

#16 Losers
      Just
      Like
      You

#12 You don't have
      A problem with me
      Don't give yourself
      That much credit

#17 Don't
      Tell
      Me
      No

#13 I don't
      Miss you
      I don't
      Miss anyone

#18 She
      Won't
      Touch
      Me

#14 My
      Friend
      Went
      Insane

#19 Don't
      Leave
      Me
      Alone

#15 I love
      Her
      She
      Shoots drugs

#20 He died unknown
      No one thought
      To look
      For his body

#21 I am
Addicted
To
Dreams

#22 Let
Go
Of
Me

#23 No
One
Has
Friends

#24 I
Can't
Help
Myself

#25 She looked at me
I shuddered
She looked away
I froze

#26 I
Write
To avoid
Myself

#27 I
Write
To confront
Myself

#28 I am well protected
Too locked up
Inside myself
To get free

#29 Embrace
Your pain
It's all
You've got

#30 The rapist
Came
Then the ambulance
Came

#31 She
     Ties off
     She shoots up
     Naked

#32 He
     Hits her
     She
     Likes it

#33 I
     Don't know
     My friends
     Do you?

#34 Ugly
     Lady
     Smoking
     Crack

#35 Car thief
     Crack dealer
     Mugger, burglar
     A lower east side
     Renaissance man

#36 No one
     Wants to
     Touch
     Her

#37 People
     Rushing
     For the train
     147 goodbyes

#38 Liars
     And
     Their
     Disease

#39 She
     Likes
     To hurt
     Me

#40 She
     Likes
     To leave
     Me

#41 She
Helps me
Hate
Myself

#46 Have
You
Ever been
Used

#42 She fell
Out a window
No one
Pushed her

#47 She was
Highly skilled
In
Self doubt

#43 Her name
Was Emily
We
Slow danced

#48 Sometimes
I still
Think of
You

#44 Cold in
New Haven
They got
Crack dealers too

#49 No
You got nothing
On
Me

#45 I want
Her
To
Touch me

#50 Stop
Staring
At my
Tits

#51 He
     Died
     Many
     Times

#52 The
     Smiling
     Woman
     Lies

#53 Count
     Your
     Friends
     Zero

#54 Don't
     Wait
     For
     Time

#55 You
     Help me
     Hate
     You

#56 That drunk
     Ran
     Over
     That dog

#57 She stares
     At her hand
     She stares
     At the gun

#58 Kid in closet
     Mom at work
     Dad in jail

#59 Kid in hell
     Mom on crack
     Dad invisible

#60 Kid in school
     Mom in kitchen
     Dad at work

#61 Kid in rehab
   Mom on mailman
   Dad in secretary

#62 Your dick is in
   Your hand
   Not in
   Her

#63 You
   Drive
   Yourself
   Insane

#64 Hey it's no problem
   Just call me
   An Asshole
   And run

#65 I can touch her
   Skin
   But I can't touch
   Her

#66 She
   Keeps
   Me
   Inside

#67 Your dick
   Is
   Too
   Small

#68 That man
   Mugged me
   Scared the hell
   Out of me

#69 That man
   Followed me
   Scared the hell
   Out of me

#70 Her
   Boyfriend
   Hit
   Me

#71 His
     New wife
     Hit
     Me

#72 My
     New brother
     Tied
     Me up

#73 Hey!
     You got
     No
     Friends

#74 We are both
     The same
     All
     Alone

#75 I am
     Searching
     For
     Emptiness

#76 Wanting to be
     Needing to be
     Dying to be
     Touched

#77 Fusion
     Is
     Satan's
     Muzak

#78 I'm
     In
     Jazz-fusion
     Hell

#79 She makes me
     Put my fist
     Through
     Glass

#80 Inside
     She
     Bleeds

#81 When I am
With you
I think
Of her

#82 Don't
Go
Yes
Do

#83 You'll
Never
Touch
Her

#84 How
Does it feel
To
Want

#85 I used to sit
In my apartment
Razor my flesh
And smell my blood

#86 Carnage
She's not
Coming
Home

#87 My father
Burnt corpse
Body
Bag

#88 My
Mother
In
Rehab

#89 Don't try
To get close
To
Me

#90 To love me
Is to
Hate
Me

#91   Kill her
        She
        Doesn't
        Exist

#92   Tonight
        I'm alone
        Freezing
        In my cell

#93   Hungry
        Freezing
        Homeless
        Maniac

#94   Humanity
        Is
        A
        Lie

#95   I made
        Her
        Smile
        Once

#96   I jerk off
        I destroy
        My need
        Of need

#97   People
        Are weak
        Push them
        Over

#98   Walk away
        Let
        It
        Burn

#99   Killing
        Himself
        For
        Her

#100   You
        Make
        Me
        Sick

#101   She's late
For work
Pregnant
And full of hate

#102   Supplication
Supplication
Endless
Supplication

#103   You
Me
The same
Strangers

#104   You
Me
The same
One of them

#105   To show me
Pain
She
Kissed me

#106   They both
Played
The
Game

#107   Jaded
Bitter
Burnt out
Broke

#108   I can't
Come back
They're all
Dead

#109   My home
Is not
Home
To me

#110   Show yourself
To me
No
Don't

#111 She taught me
   All I know
   About wanting
   To die

#112 She fills
   The room
   With light
   And grace

#113 I like her
   So much
   I hide
   From her

#114 That dude
   Came at me
   With a
   Golf club

#115 Out here
   There's no noise
   Besides
   Gunshots & sirens

#116 Let me be
   Nice to you
   I will
   Pay you

#117 My
   Smile
   Is
   Broken

#118 At night
   I see
   Her
   Face

#119 She
   Never
   Got over
   Me

#120 Tonight
   Swallows
   Me
   Whole

#121 16 years old
      Are geniuses
      A dime a dozen
      Then they screw it up

#122 My fear
      Justifies
      My
      Thoughts

#123 I need you
      But I can't
      Tell you
      That

#124 She won't
      Touch me
      I feel
      Dirty

#125 My
      Thoughts
      Are
      Aliens

#126 My
      Dreams
      Hate
      Me

#127 I
      Hate
      Myself
      To sleep

#128 She was
      His drug
      Heroin
      Was hers

#129 The first handful
      Of clay
      On her son's
      Pine box

#130 You're
      Going
      To
      Die

#131 Reduced
To
Begging for
Food money

#132 The boys
In the men's room
Baiting
Faggots

#133 Dealers howling
All night long
Train kept rolling
All night long

#134 She
Loves me
I
Don't care

#135 The
Poison
In
Lies

#136 He looked at her
Something
Turned cancerous
He was in love

#137 Those
Streets
Pure
Disease

#138 Uneaten food
In the garbage
Unfed people
In the street

#139 She is magic
I blinked my eyes
Presto!
My wallet was gone

#140 The cabbie waits
For his fare
To buy
Some crack

#141 Cancer
As
A
Rule

#142 Weakness
Over
Powers
Me

#143 I
Lie
Like
You

#144 He would
Do anything
To get
Laid

#145 I
Wish
I could
Burn

#146 I love you
But
Not like
I used to

#147 In magic moments
My hands
Turn into
Fists

#148 I lied
I told her
That
I loved her

#149 Help
Me
Hurt
You

#150 I keep
The truth
From
Myself

#151 I hated
      You
      From
      The start

#152 I am
      The
      Alienation
      Machine

#153 The man sits
      2 hours to go
      Then
      The electric chair

#154 Leave
      Me
      Now
      Forever

#155 She
      Is
      Walking
      Death

#156 Your life
      Is
      Nothing
      To me

#157 Reach out
      I won't
      Be there
      For you

#158 Bus driver
      Driving
      Under the influence
      Of hate

#159 Peace
      Makes me
      Want to
      Kill

#160 I am
      The all night
      Pure burning
      Hate

#161 I'm
Addicted
To
Everything

#162 She calls me
Up
I hang her
Up

#163 I
Laugh
In
Your face

#164 I will
Hurt you
If you
Let me

#165 His
Love
Is
Destructive

#166 She
Was warned
Now
She's dead

#167 That kid
Rolls joints
Just like
His father

#168 Mother
Father
Son
Junkies

#169 Coat hanger
Septic infection
Pain until death
City morgue

#170 I'm not telling a lie
She shoots speed
I'm in love
With her

#171   Doing
       Lunch
       With
       Jesus

#172   The streets
       Heat up
       War is
       Here

#173   My
       Dad
       Raped
       Mom

#174   I
       Am
       Ultimate
       Addiction

#175   Youth
       I had it
       And then
       Lost it

#176   He shot
       Her
       He got
       Away

#177   Two
       Raped
       On
       Campus

#178   AIDS
       Pass
       It
       On

#179   You
       Are
       Already
       Dead

#180   I can't
       Control
       My
       Rage

#181 She touched me
Here
I punched her
There

#182 He went
For years
Without
Sanity

#183 There's
Nothing
Here
For me

#184 She
Spat
On
Me

#185 The uncompromising
Will
To
Destroy

#186 The
War
Is all
I have

#187 At
War
With
God

#188 She got raped
She got killed
She got tagged
She got buried

#189 Kids at the loony bin
Have sharp eyes
Sharp teeth
Twisted hearts

#190 When those boys
Beat me up
I wanted to kill
The whole race

#191 She
Slept
With
Me

#192 She holds
Her breath
And
Kisses me

#193 She has
Blue eyes
How they
Lie

#194 I want
To taste
Her
Body

#195 No friends
No hope
No
Sweat

#196 All the way
To the jungle
Half way
Back home

#197 I know
She lies and steals
She's
A junky

#198 He came home
From work
Used
Again

#199 The good times
Drove him
To
Insanity

#200 Hell
Is
Like
This

#201 Send
God
Back
Home

#206 Bury my dad
I don't care
That he's
Not dead

#202 Cop
Dying
Me
Laughing

#207 She could
Fuck me
Or kill me
I wouldn't care

#203 Oh
No
Raped
Again

#208 Here
Comes
Big
Disease

#204 Third night
Of spring
Sun slowed down
Moon took its time

#209 Places
For
People
Like me

#205 Summer
Means
Random
Shootings

#210 Nothing
To
Hope
For

#211 Suicide
Was
Her
Friend

#216 Bladed
Hot
Black
Night

#212 It was all
I had
Now it's
Gone

#217 I
Lick
Her
Stomach

#213 Summer's
Almost
Here
Good!

#218 I
Am
Total
War

#214 Shoot me
Into
Your
Veins

#219 I
Forgot
My
Addiction

#215 Torched
In
His
Cell

#220 Starving
For love
Almost
Dead

#221 Fireworks
When
I touch
Her

#226 After
Hate
There's
Nothing

#222 No
Way
But
Forward

#227 She lied
To everyone
Who ever
Loved her

#223 Moving violation:
In one ear
And
Out the other

#228 No
One
Like
Me

#224 Her eyes
Her hands
Please
Don't stop

#229 She treated
Herself
Like
Garbage

#225 She
Dries
Like
Honey

#230 My body
Is
My
Enemy

#231 My body
      Is trying
      To kill
      Me

#232 It's 4:00 am
      Denny's is full
      People talking
      About drinking

#233 She
      Makes
      My eyes
      Revolt

#234 Some people
      Shouldn't live
      People like
      Daryl Gates

#235 No woman
      Makes me
      Feel anything
      Anymore

#236 I miss
      The feeling
      Of missing
      You

#237 I tried to
      Touch her
      She spat
      On me

#238 Everyday
      I'm closer
      To
      Death

#239 The man
      Kisses
      The boy
      Not me

#240 14 year old boy
      Machine gun
      In his
      Hands

#241 When depression
Comes down
I swear
My bones crack

#242 Her teeth
Knocked out
Sing a
Sad song

#243 The man
On the street
In the snow
Hard cold raw deal

#244 He was
So stupid
He was
In line

#245 No one
Will help
You when
You're helpless

#246 Tell me
How it feels
When the needle
Goes in

#247 She loved
Sex
He loved
Her

#248 I can't
Find
My
Self

#249 When
Will
I
Die

#250 10 years
Thrown away
San Quentin
Prison

#251   Feed
People
To
People

#252   Life
A
Constant
Rape

#253   Can you
Touch me
So I can
Feel it

#254   Don't
Mess
With
Desperation

#255   His
Veins
Were
Screaming

#256   End it
Let it
Fall
Down

#257   Soon
Everything
Will be
The same

#258   Cigarettes
Sweat
And
Guilt

#259   I never knew
Hate
Until I met
Her

#260   Hate
Keeps
Me
Alive

#261 Napalm
I Can
Smell
Victory

#262 You're
A
Human
Joke

#263 You don't
Make me
Feel
Anything

#264 The older I get
The less I want
Soon
I will leave you

#265 I don't
Hold on
Good
Bye

#266 The
Dead
Still
Walk

#267 Cracked lip girl
Wants to fuck me
50 Bucks
Room included

#268 He turned the corner
They were waiting
For him
What a coincidence

#269 That
Guy
On
Death Row

#270 Pulling
Hard
Towards
Death

#271   I love them
       Then
       I cut them
       Up

#272   He was
       Destroyed by
       His own
       Kind

#273   Over weight
       $30.00 tie die shirt
       Rich girl
       Bummer

#274   She said
       I shouldn't do it
       I couldn't do it
       If I wanted to

#275   15 years
       In
       A
       Cell

#276   Cage makers
       Human impersonators
       God almighty
       Pulls their strings

#277   I undressed
       She lit a cigarette
       And watched
       Hungry

#278   Kill
       For
       The
       Taste

#279   The
       Earth
       Is
       Burning

#280   Too late
       Late
       To
       Learn

#281 You
Die
Life
Lives

#286 They
Like me
They are not
Like me

#282 Driven
Insane
Totally
Driven

#287 I don't know
Friends
From
Strangers

#283 You
Are
Not
Tough

#288 Are
You
My
Friend?

#284 I
Don't
Love
You

#289 Can
I
Trust
You?

#285 I
Can
Use
You

#290 Will
You
Leave
Me?

#291 I have
      A home
      It's called
      War

#292 I have a
      Woman
      I love her
      She is war

#293 I have a
      Reason
      Barrel in
      My mouth

#294 Broke in the house
      Raped
      The retarded
      Girl

#295 All
      Life
      Was
      Destroyed

#296 Summer
      Nights
      Spent well
      Stalking and killing

#297 Moonless
      Night
      Breaking
      Black

#298 Two
      Bodies
      Sweating
      Together

#299 He came home
      She was
      Not
      Alone

#300 People
      Make
      Me
      Confused

#301 I
      Wait
      For
      Summer

#302 Let
      Me
      Hurt
      You

#303 She touched him
      She showed her
      She took him
      From her

#304 You
      Me
      Rooftop
      Tonight

#305 Sweat
      Her hair
      Sticking
      To me

#306 Insanity
      Waits
      For
      Me

#307 Pushers
      Unite!
      Unionize
      Organize

#308 She
      Made him
      Into a
      Human wreck

#309 She turned
      Away
      I threw myself
      Away

#310 At the end
      That's all
      There
      Is

#311 The
Single
Bullet
Cure

#316 He
Saw
Her head
Explode

#312 The night
She touched him
He relived it
For years

#317 My
Father
Drowning
Puppies

#313 I
Need
My
Hate

#318 They stood
In line
To fuck
Her

#314 Father
Cigar smoke
Screaming
Oaths

#319 In summer nights
Dreams
Are
Real

#315 He
Put the gun
In
His mouth

#320 Touch me
Watch me
Destroy
Myself

#321 I leave you
      Now
      You leave me
      Cold

#322 He
      Inhaled
      My
      Fist

#323 The man sits
      Waiting
      To be
      Gassed

#324 In my dreams
      I kill you
      Over
      And over

#325 I
      Hate
      This
      Place

#326 Her
      Laugh
      Destroyed
      Me

#327 Low
      Opinions
      Run
      High

#328 She never
      Got out
      Of the
      Ghetto

#329 Suicide
      He got
      It
      Right

#330 Tell
      Me
      About
      Power

#331 The end
Of the world
Let's do it
Come on

#332 Pull
Down
That
Trigger

#333 Soldiers
Dying
In
War

#334 Animal
Numbered
Cataloged
Caged

#335 I'm alone
Riding
The
Roads

#336 Touch
Me
I'm
Dying

#337 Green
Time
Summer
Explosion

#338 Summer
Nights
Defy
Time

#339 No
Time
Like
Life time

#340 Mom
Hits me
If she keeps up
I will kill her

#341 Everything
She says
Is a
Lie

#342 Her
Orgasms
Were
Fake

#343 Living
On
An
Excuse

#344 Land
Lord
Almighty
God living

#345 Hold
My
Hand
Please

#346 Hold
My
Gun
Please

#347 He made
Excuses
He made
Lies

#348 The
Night
Destroys
Me

#349 She got
Raped for
A
Living

#350 I
Come
Real
Cheap

#351 I stare
At her chest
I can't help
Myself

#352 I know
What you
Like
Don't I

#353 She took it
Hard
He took it
And split

#354 The boy
Left home
He never
Came back

#355 Dangerous
Desperate
Destructive
Beauty

#356 No one
Can help you
Like I can
Hurt you

#357 You need
Pain
You need
Me

#358 I can't
Help
My
Addiction

#359 Can you feel
Cold greasy
Fear
Touching you

#360 The man
Denied his check
Limps back
To the bus stop

#361 Veterans:
They're
Still
Killing you

#366 Don't
Wait
For
Death

#362 Wake up
Smell
The
Napalm

#367 Don't
Worry
I'm
Coming

#363 My
Love
Dismantles
Women

#368 Crack house
Rocking out
All night
Like 7-11

#364 I left
Her
In
Pieces

#369 The boss
Hated
Feared
Needed

#365 That man
Heart smasher
Home wrecker
Sex god

#370 At work
She shoots up
In the toilet
Another junky

#371 Her
Apathetic
Down south
Eyes

#376 Blood
On
My
Pillow

#372 She shot
A hole in the wall
She was
Just joking

#377 I
Sleep
Alone
Always

#373 I
Died alone
In
My room

#378 Drugs
Are
My
Life

#374 So
Easy
To forget
You

#379 Business men
Lie daily
So do
You

#375 Mississippi
Violent
Heart
Break

#380 Do
You
Feel
Lucky

#381 I
Gave her
All
My problems

#386 My woman
My gun
My
God

#382 She taught him
To
Shoot
Smack

#387 She shot
Up
She shot
Her son

#383 17 years old
He shot himself
In the attic
I miss him

#388 The world
Is weak
Let's
Burn it

#384 Your eyes
Make me
Blind
Touch me

#389 I make
You take
I break
You fake

#385 I
Am
Long
Dead

#390 Life
Is
A
Disease

#391   Her legs
       Black stocking
       Her smile
       She walks away

#392   She kissed
       Him
       She punched
       Me

#393   He finished
       Basic training
       He started
       Drinking

#394   Busted
       For
       Smoking
       Dust

#395   Real war
       South
       Central
       LA

#396   Come
       And
       Hit
       Me

#397   I
       Will
       Destroy
       You

#398   He sits
       In the park
       Drinking beer
       Reliving Vietnam

#399   Old woman
       Head
       In
       Stove

#400   I got
       A million
       Sad
       Stories

#401 Standing in line
At the
Rape
Crisis center

#402 Swinging
Waiting
For
Death

#403 She tries
So hard
To hurt
Me

#404 The
Endless
Mind
Fuck

#405 Her
Post
Abortion
Blues

#406 I can't
Make
Her
Come

#407 She can't
Make
Me
Cry

#408 Ghetto
Superman
Flying
PCP

#409 Looking
For
A
Stranger

#410 She killed me
Over
And
Over

#411   Loneliness
        Is
        My
        Friend

#412   She
        Claws
        Her
        Face

#413   South America?
        Central America?
        South Central
        LA

#414   Life is
        A
        Social
        Disease

#415   I've
        Got
        Your
        Fear

#416   Come
        And
        Get
        It

#417   Me and her
        Destroying
        Each other
        For free

#418   Pigs
        Playing
        Pig
        Games

#419   Highway
        Cat mouse
        Pig machine
        Retard

#420   Pigs
        Human
        Gods
        And me

#421 I put it
In the pig's mouth
And cleared
His throat

#422 I have
Bad dreams
I buy
And sell

#423 Raped
And
Beaten
Again

#424 I asked
Her name
She laughed
And left

#425 I
Am
A
Coward

#426 Sullen
Sunken eyed
Burning arm
With a Salem

#427 3 years in
Jail
Made him
A criminal

#428 The war
Is over
For those
Who lie

#429 Child
At the
Bottom
Of the pool

#430 Young
Girl
Lying
Punctured

#431 Your
Daughter
Tastes
Good

#432 Tonight
Another
City
Dies

#433 The
Fields
Of
Pain

#434 She shot me
Up
I shot her
Down

#435 She's
Not
Alive
Anymore

#436 She
Is
Killing
Me

#437 Tears
Come
Broken
Teeth

#438 Bitterly
Spitting
Rapist
Cum

#439 Dreams
From
Father's
Hell

#440 Her
Mouth
His
Home

#441 She
Always
Hurts
Me

#442 Teen
Aged
Hate
Machine

#443 I dream
Of her
To this
Day

#444 I
Hate
My
Face

#445 Love
Left
Me
Empty

#446 Why do you lie
Look at me
Hey I'm talking
To you

#447 The infant
Thrown from
The fifth floor
Couldn't fly

#448 Born
Raised
Disciplined
Destroyed

#449 The path
To her heart
Covered
With scars

#450 He got
Good at
Getting
Used

#451 Drunk
      Dead
      Burning
      Car

#452 Crying
      Father
      At
      Funeral

#453 He's
      Dead
      That's
      It

#454 I can't
      Forget you
      I wish
      I could

#455 My
      Hate
      Is
      God

#456 He shot his
      Mother
      He shot his
      Father

#457 He shot his
      Wife
      He shot his
      Son

#458 She
      Shot
      Them
      All

#459 Tell me
      Why
      I love
      You

#460 Here
      Is
      The
      Gun

#461 Hey punk
Check
This
Out

#462 Free
Love
Hippie
Machine

#463 The
Horror
Of
Violence

#464 15 years old
Sawed off
Shot gun
In tow

#465 I
Can't
Bleed
Anymore

#466 I tore myself
Away from her
I tore myself
Apart

#467 He got
Lost in
Her
Love hate game

#468 She drove
The family
To drink
And destruction

#469 She touched
Me
She scarred
Me

#470 My head
Is a
Room full
Of headaches

#471 I
      Rent
      Good
      Times

#472 The old man
      Alone in the room
      Listening to water
      Drip in the sink

#473 The bottle
      Was
      His
      Life

#474 Her time is
      Short
      The cancer is
      Spreading

#475 I am filled
      With love
      Drugs
      And money

#476 He lost
      His wife
      She lost
      Her mind

#477 There's nothing
      Like
      Burning
      Hate

#478 The ghetto
      Singing
      To me
      Tonight

#479 I
      Give
      Her
      Fear

#480 Filling holes
      Filling gaps
      Passing time
      Killing ourselves

#481   She says
       The needle
       Chases her
       And keeps up

#482   Walking
       Hand in hand
       To
       Rehab

#483   She
       Keeps
       Me
       Hanging

#484   Her
       Lies
       Cut
       Me

#485   She tried
       To talk
       To me
       I'm deaf

#486   Your smile
       Doesn't mean
       A thing
       To me

#487   I'm
       Alone
       In my
       Cage

#488   I
       Am
       Real
       Animal

#489   The girls
       Surrounded him
       Talking and touching
       I watched

#490   He's good
       At having
       Nothing
       To say

#491 I tell
My junky girl
All my
Problems

#492 Who
Can I
Turn
To

#493 I'm safe
In my
Own arms
Self possessed

#494 Too
Strong
To
Die

#495 Too
Numb
To
Feel

#496 Too
Hateful
To
Hate

#497 I'm
High
On
Hate

#498 My
Mom
Smokes
Dust

#499 I'm a
Freak
Touch
Me

#500 No
Time
Rotten
Life

#501 I
Drop
Fire
Bombs

#506 Man in car
Mean smile
Waiting
For you

#502 She came
From hell
Smack dealing
Lying bitch

#507 Honey
Your pusher
Called you
Honey

#503 If you want
Peace
Go fill the streets
With blood

#508 The needle
Is
My
God

#504 You
Are
Killing
Earth

#509 Too
Much
Too
Late

#505 No
Place
Like
War

#510 Strong
Inside
My
Self

#511 I
    Have
    Nothing
    But me

#512 She turned to me
    Eyes and mouth
    Slightly open
    Warm breath

#513 A needle
    For
    Every
    Vein

#514 Life
    Sentenced
    Thrown
    Away

#515 She cried
    Black summer night
    Right eye swollen
    Jaw wired shut

#516 He jumped
    No one
    Told him
    He couldn't fly

#517 Tell me how
    It feels
    When the gun
    Is in your hands

#518 My hand is so cold
    It's going to break off
    If these cabs
    Keep passing me by

#519 Touch me
    I'll pay you
    Lie to me
    Tell me you mean it

#520 I gave her all in me
    Clearly
    It was not
    Enough

#521   Don't put that gun
To your head
We aren't done
With you yet

#522   Speeding
Like a bullet
Falling
Like a tear

#523   Horror
Paralyzed velocity
Car crash
Broken body

#524   Alcohol
Helped him
Keep the dreams
From invading his sleep

#525   One seat open
At the back of the bus
I am
Too scared to go

#526   Teenage boy
Hanging in the garage
Wait until your father
Comes home

#527   Jewel eyed
Cruel mouth
I think
I'm in love

#528   Her flesh
Sagging slightly
Underneath my hands
I shut my eyes and lie

#529   Late night
I look out my window
Snow falls past
The crime lights

#530   I
Have
Killer
Instinct

#531 I only smile
At children
They need it
The most

#532 He sits
On the porch
Maybe today
He dies

#533 He
Lives
He
Rapes

#534 I
Am
A slave
To time

#535 He sits in his room
All is quiet
The night moves
Slow and endless

#536 I can't ask her
What her name is
I can't make
My mouth work

#537 He shot
His wife
And watched
MTV

#538 Alone
At
The
Bar

#539 His father went
To the gas chamber
His mother went
To the liquor store

#540 He beat off again
Same place
Same time
Same reason

#541 His sister cries
She hates it
When he shoots up
In the bathroom

#542 He went out
To drink
He came back
Too drunk

#543 He looks
Through
Prison bars
Wasted life

#544 She passed out
When
They put the sheet
Over his face

#545 Clear autumn night
Cool breeze
Bright moon
Magic!

#546 She and I walked
Down the sidewalk
Leaves crunching
Beneath our feet

#547 She became
Famous on our block
After some dude
Raped her

#548 She turned
And kissed him
He turned
Electric

#549 Breathe in
Wood burning fire
Street light glow
Autumn night

#550 She smiled
At me tonight
Where is she
Now

#551 Hey mister pilot
Turn around
I left something
Back there

#552 McArthur Blvd
In the fall
Damn!
Missed it again

#553 Hi I
Deal drugs
To your
Sister

#554 She wants
Him not you
Doesn't that make
You want to kill

#555 The dog
Carries
The leash
To the master

#556 Waiting for the bus
She's late
For
A twelve hour shift

#557 Three years
He's been dead
Still
It hurts me so

#558 There was nowhere
He could go
So he went
There

#559 Sometimes the world
Kisses you cheek
But not tonight
Not here

#560 Lonely night
On
Death Row
Tonight

#561
She told him
That she didn't want
To touch him
Anymore

#562
At the job
Looks at the clock
Looks back down
6 1/2 hours to go

#563
The sound
Of his voice
Brought
Me down

#564
I wish I had the guts
To let go
Of what is
Killing me

#565
Real love
A
Real turn off
Jaded bastard

#566
Walking up
31st street
On a fall night
Is worth the wait

#567
His hand slips
The whiskey bottle
Falls and shatters
He starts to cry

#568
The light go down
The people file out
The performer slumps
Empty and alone

#569
He checks the mailbox
Empty
He sits back down
Stares at his shoes

#570
I think
He needs
A
Break

#571 The judge said
Six years
The judged thought
He was dreaming

#572 I'm a
Slave
To my
Insecurity

#573 He tried to cry
The tears
Wouldn't
Come

#574 The girls
Made him
Feel
Filthy

#575 You know
That feeling
When you
Lie

#576 Go ahead
Touch me
I wish
You would

#577 The car
Hit
The boy
Perfectly

#578 My father
Drinks
He scares
Me

#579 He picks up
The phone
And holds it
Puts it back down

#580 Won't
You
Ever
Stop?

#581 Please
I can't
Take it
Anymore

#582 No one
Listens
To me
Anymore

#583 Sad
Stupid
Raped
And stoned

#584 When
She touched him
He felt
Cold and distant

#585 He's drunk
Again
And
It hurts

#586 Jealousy
Eats my
Brain
Like acid

#587 She told me
How her father
Used to
Feel her up

#588 The telephone
Turned into
His
Enemy

#589 Those nights
Long ago
Where
The best

#590 He threw up
On himself
Again
Awesome!

#591 She was
Hated
Amongst
Her friends

#596 The sound
Of autumn
Wind
Dead leaves

#592 I never
Got
Over
Her

#597 Please
Let
Me
Go

#593 His
Fist
Hits
The glass

#598 Girl
High
On
Heroin

#594 His
Fist
Hits
The woman

#599 Boy
Low
On
Heartbreak

#595 His
Fist
Hits
The child

#600 The wino's face
A study
In
Pain

#601   He
      Kissed her
      She
      Started crying

#606   She
      Caught
      Him
      Looking

#602   Don't
      Trust
      Them
      Really

#607   The cop asked
      He forgot
      How
      To talk

#603   He took
      A deep breath
      Gripped his pistol
      And entered
      The liquor store

#608   He hasn't seen
      Her
      For
      Months

#604   He came
      With the bat
      He meant
      Business

#609   She ran
      Her hand
      Up
      His shirt

#605   Monday alarm
      5:30 am ringing
      Relentless loud
      Ice cold room

#610   He took off
      His glasses
      He made
      A fist

#611 Child
Abuse
From
Hell

#612 That bird
That sings
At 3:00 am
Sings to me

#613 He approaches
The electric chair
The priest
Coughs

#614 Don't worry pal
We are
Right behind
You

#615 She is amazing
No one
Can make me feel
Worse

#616 Beautiful
Young
Hooked
On heroin

#617 She loved
Him
It
Wounded her

#618 Shut that dog
Up
Or I'll
Kill it

#619 They move
They feel
Immortal
They are

#620 She stares
She smiles
She walks
Away

#621 She
Shot
Her
Self

#626 He's
Talking loud
At the back
Of the bus

#622 Hate
Fear
Bullets
Fists

#626 The old man
Falls down
We all
Walk by

#623 Agent Orange
Scars
His
Skin

#628 The blood
In a puddle
Drying on
Sunset Blvd

#624 You
Want it
So
Bad

#629 Even
Nobody
Knows
Me

#625 The woman
Lights up
Waits
For the bus

#630 The city
Slams
My
Guts

#631 She's not
On
His
Mind

#632 My mother
Got mugged
So
What

#633 In
The
End
Oh!

#634 Wipe
That
Smile
Off

#635 She's
Dead
Me
Too

#636 Holding
Her
Broken
Hands

#637 Piles
Of
Bodies
Rotting

#638 I
Could see
The end
With her

#639 That child
That mirror
That stare
That monster

#640 She can't
Hurt me
Yes
She can

#641 I love you
Because
It pays
The rent

#646 Man lying
In garbage
Man lying
In hell

#642 He had
No respect
She had
No limit

#647 Police
Are
Not
Human

#643 She
Crawled
For
Him

#648 She
Found
The secret
To feeling pain

#644 Mean
Abusive
Forceful
Father

#649 I'm dead now
Can you
Help me
Love

#645 Ugly woman
Whiskey breath
Walking talking
Death machine

#650 My woman
Is in
My
Head

#651   6 hours
       In
       The
       Closet

#656   Once
       A junky
       Always
       A junky

#652   Locked
       In a room
       Listening to
       Mother screw

#657   She destroys
       Men
       I am
       A boy

#653   Not as it
       Seems
       She smiles
       And lies

#658   My
       Mother
       Will
       Burn

#654   Go
       Start
       A
       War

#659   My
       Father
       Is
       Not

#655   Go
       Start
       A
       Band

#660   She told
       Her friends
       Lies about
       Me

#661 Who
Fucks
The
Retarded boy

#662 Virgins
Explode
In
Head-on!

#663 He
Brakes
For
Drunks

#664 He
Prays
For
Salvation

#665 He
Begs
For
Forgiveness

#666 Joe
Cole's
Area
Code

#667 He
Scares
His
Wife

#668 He
Hates
His
Life

#669 He
Fears
His
Boss

#670 He
Gets
In
Line

#671 He's
On
His
Way

#672 Tell me
How it feels
When the knife
Is in your guts

#673 With all
That is in me
I long for you
Overman

#674 She passed me
In the street
Every part of her
Smiled

#675 You sit
I sit
We lie
To ourselves

#676 She
Touched him
She was
Destroyed

#677 Her laughter
Sounded like
Glass
Breaking

#678 Do you
Smoke?
No, do you
Fuck?

#679 Come on
Get out
Of that car
I'll kill you

#680 It had been
So long
He forgot what
It was like

#681 I inhale her
      Perfume
      From my shirt
      I expand

#682 He kissed
      Her neck
      His knees
      Went weak

#683 I can't
      Pay
      What am I
      Going to do

#684 He hated
      Himself
      When
      He drank

#685 He shoots
      The meth
      Nods to his friends
      Good stuff

#686 His father drank
      His father yelled
      His father beat
      His kids

#687 Hot summer
      Nights
      Stars
      Staring down

#688 Be good
      Because tonight
      I manufacture
      Your dreams

#689 I see her
      I can't
      Help
      It

#690 She looks
      At him
      His heart
      Rises

#691　Don't tell
　　　Me
　　　About
　　　Love

#692　Fat lady
　　　In her uniform
　　　Limps to the diner
　　　Late for work again

#693　The bum
　　　Vomits
　　　Wine, food
　　　Blood

#694　Touch me
　　　I'm
　　　Dying
　　　To Death

#695　I don't know you
　　　I don't love you
　　　I don't hate you
　　　Yet

#696　She sits
　　　At the bus stop
　　　She vomits
　　　And sleeps

#697　In my dreams
　　　Everyone
　　　Is
　　　A junky

#698　His fist
　　　Found a home
　　　In her
　　　Mouth

#699　Some times
　　　I don't know
　　　If I can
　　　Take it

#700　The child screams
　　　In
　　　Real
　　　Pain

#701 You hate yourself
I
Like
That

#702 The junkie
Flexes and waits
For you
To walk by

#703 Her
Breath
Stinks
Cheap wine

#704 He
Lights
Another
Joint

#705 He
Learned
To
Suck

#706 Tonight
I
Burn
On earth

#707 Another
Fuck
Another
Life

#708 He hit
His mom
He felt
Nothing

#709 Endless
Night
Summer
Hell

#710 Work
Fills
My
Life

#711 Clouds
Fill
My
Prison sky

#712 Blood
Fills
My
Heart

#713 Dirt
Fills
My
Grave

#714 Hurry
Up
End
It

#715 Summer's
Furnace
Burning
Me

#716 The woman
His reason
To shoot
Himself

#717 I know you
I love you
I'll show you
I'll kill you

#718 Summer!
The
Black
Leech

#719 Black
Oven
In
NYC

#720 Dying
Over
And
Over

#721 Crushed
Like
An
Insect

#722 I
Am
Your
Answer

#723 I see her
Looking good
Walking away
From me

#724 Going
To
Work
Again

#725 They
Fight
All
Night

#726 The woman
In my dreams
Touched me
I'm burning

#727 Late
Night
Hole
I'm descending

#728 Coughing up
Black dreams
Memories
Dead blood

#729 Endless
Hate
I'm
King

#730 My
Dreams
Draw
Blood

#731 I hate
      The world
      Low life
      Creeps

#732 My life
      I can't
      Wait
      To terminate

#733 When
      I see
      Her
      I ignite

#734 She buys
      Drugs
      She sells
      Heaven

#735 One
      More
      Abortion
      Blues

#736 A world
      Of pain
      Full of
      Love

#737 I am
      The
      Abused
      Children

#738 Tie off
      Shoot up
      Get off
      Pass out

#739 He got
      His wings
      Flying high
      On glue

#740 Bathing
      In
      Her
      Tears

#741 This
Is
Real
Hell

#742 No
Chance
To
Escape

#743 Say
Goodbye
To
Missouri

#744 Men
Grow
Into
Boys

#745 When I saw her
Chop that line
I swore off
Drugs and women

#746 His hobby
Is
Child and wife
Abuse

#747 Your
Wife
Fools
Around

#748 Your
Husband
Fools
Around

#749 Fools
Can't
Help
Themselves

#750 Life:
One
Long
Rape

#751 Summer's here
I'll kill
Each night
I swear

#752 The inferno
Throw me in
I want to know
What love is

#753 She pulled
The shade down
She pulled
The trigger down

#754 My mother
Drunk
At my
Birthday party

#755 His father's
Vice
Was
Advice

#756 Chain smoking
Sex partners
Burned her out
Human ash tray

#757 Child parts
In the dumpster
Ah!
Young love

#758 You broke
My heart
I'll break
Your arm

#759 Even god
Can't stop
Bullets
Ha ha ha

#760 Bang!
Yes
Better
Already

#761
Frozen
Train ride
Lost children
Bleeding

#762
He came
Home
King of
Vietnam

#763
Feelings
Let
Me
Down

#764
Emotions
Twist
My
Soul

#765
Too easy
To get
Destroyed
Cha cha cha

#766
He got lost
In his head
Thought he was
In the jungle

#767
How's the book?
Hate me yet?
Keep reading
You fuck head

#768
Car
Crashes
Are
Magic

#769
She swore
His tongue
Was from
Hell

#770
Getting
Good
At
Lying

#771 Death
Commands
My
Life

#772 He went
To meet
His makers
He shot ma and pa

#773 Her shirt
See through
My smile
See through

#774 The gun
The man
The shot
The legend

#775 She played
The game
She got
Destroyed

#776 They beat
His
Dumb ass
Flat

#777 She
Swallows
Men's
Souls

#778 Right
Before
The fist
Hit

#779 Grinding
On
The
Roof

#780 Your girl
Under
Your friend
Walk away

#781 No
      Angels
      In
      LA

#782 But
      Pigs
      Drive
      Cars

#783 And
      Money
      Really
      Talks

#784 My sister
      Sells
      My brother's
      Dick

#785 Nothing
      But
      A
      Junky

#786 I know
      Dead junkies
      But no
      Ex junkies

#787 I'm heroin
      Rollins
      Hates
      Me

#788 I'm coke
      Rollins
      Is
      Killing me

#789 I'm truth
      I
      love
      Rollins

#790 I'm
      Death
      I'm
      Faithful

#791 It's
War time
At
All times

#792 Who
Is
A real
Artist?

#793 She
Plays
My
Soul

#794 Her
Mother's
Collapsed
Veins

#795 Far from home
Lone cold hungry
Raped in jail
Tears and blood

#796 Mom
On crack
She waits
For death

#797 Hardened
By
Whoring
And heroin

#798 NYC
Tonight
Love
Hate

#799 God
Died
In
Brooklyn

#800 Lightnin'
Born in Texas
Raised on blues
Alive in hell

#801 Friends
      Liars
      Lovers
      Enemies

#802 All my
      Women
      Have had
      Abortions

#803 Death
      Is
      Like
      South Central LA

#804 Roaches
      High
      On
      Suicide

#805 NYC
      Is
      A
      Disease

#806 Hold on
      Tight dear
      The car
      Is crashing

#807 Raped in
      The back
      Of a
      Greyhound bus

#808 My
      Brother
      Is a
      Woman

#809 17
      Year
      Old
      Killer

#810 Terminal
      Rape
      LA
      County

#811 He lied
It's the
Only thing
He liked

#816 Her mouth
Filled up
With something
Good

#812 I
Am
A
Serious artist

#817 I'm not
Sorry
That I'm not
Sorry

#813 The whole family
Jumped
Off the roof
I laughed

#818 Pain
Taught
Him
Respect

#814 The kid
Drank dad's
Gasoline
I laughed

#819 Pain
Taught
Him
Fear

#815 I am
The
Product of
Domestic strife

#820 Pain
Taught
Him
Hate

#821 The
Road
Is
Teacher

#826 She
Leeches
My
Soul

#822 They threw her
Off the roof
She didn't die
But she was upset

#827 That kid
Died
People say
I did it

#823 Old man
Asleep on
Subway
Time to die

#828 High
In jail
Low on
Resources

#824 Their father
Beat sense
In and out
Of them

#829 Blind
Raping
The
Dead

#825 Oh!
The
Nimble
Junkie

#830 After the drugs
The fire
In his eyes
Died

#831   Plastic
Like
My
Soul

#832   The
Drugs
Killed
Her

#833   Crack
Fallen face
Young woman
Looking hard

#834   Another kid
Shot dead
Do you care
Well do you?

#835   That girl
Was untouchable
I hated
Her

#836   She had sex
With me
It made
Her laugh

#837   He is evil
He brings
Pain home
To his family

#838   Girl in the
Trunk
Sick in the
Head

#839   If man was
Born to kill
God would have...
Whoops

#840   Her baby
Was born
A junky
How sweet

#841 Twin whores
In Minneapolis
Found dead
In hotel room

#842 He drinks
And cries
And vomits
And drinks

#843 My world!
Oh! oh!
My world!
Oh god!

#844 Fill
Those
Body bags
Boys!

#845 He
Rapes
Old
Women

#846 Sick
Of love
Sick
Of lies

#847 Slashed
Her wrist
In her room
The carpet's history

#848 If a pretty
Girl jumps off
The roof
Will she float

#849 Young
Blonde
Splattered
Porsche 914

#850 Alienated
From
His
Body

#851   First night
       Married
       Double bed
       Double suicide

#852   Party
       After
       The
       Funeral

#853   He got his
       Information from
       The receiving end
       Of a joint

#854   Started out
       Strong
       Ended up
       On pot

#855   Get away
       Don't touch
       I hate you
       Divorce me

#856   I'm so cold
       I cry ice
       I'm so bad
       I shoot crack

#857   Hey
       Let's go
       Shoot some
       Crack dealers

#858   Heroin
       Girl
       Wooden
       Heart

#859   No way
       To treat
       Your slave
       Too cruel

#860   If he
       Shot himself
       I would
       Respect him

#861 Twice
Divorced
Never
Again

#862 Miami
Whore
Washed up
In the surf

#863 Speed
Kills
Right?
Right

#864 I should
Have my
Bodyguard
Rape you

#865 They
Beat
The
Retarded kid

#866 Make him
Weak
Make him
Pray

#867 Make him
Watch
Me
Rape her

#868 He
Entered
Her...
House

#869 Nazi
This
Nazi
That

#870 No one came
To the wedding
No one came
To the funeral

#871 Hail
Joe Cole
Hail
Mitch Bury

#876 Foul mouthed
Women
Speak highly
Of me

#872 Life
Peaks
Early
On

#877 L-iving
I-n
F-ear
E-veryday

#873 Enjoy
Your
Youth
Now

#878 Hey son
You're drafted
Hey son
You're busted

#874 Older
People
Are from
Mars

#879 17 years old
Soldier
Virgin
Dead

#875 I'm becoming
Old
Like
Elvis

#880 H-e
E-ntered
L-ove's
L-ie

#881 Time
Causes
All
Wounds

#886 Bled
To Death
In the
Back seat

#882 I
Was
Alive
Once

#887 Born
In a barn
Raised
In jail

#883 No I don't
Love you
No I don't
Love me

#888 Dead man
Till death
Till death
Till death

#884 She
Was
Self
Employed

#889 She shot herself
At her
Senior prom
After party

#885 She
Was
Self
Rejected

#890 A
Marriage
Like
Death

#891 Pull
The trigger
Help me
Out

#896 Take
My
Face
Away

#892 Endless
Homeless
Penniless
Immaculate

#897 When
He died
I was
Overjoyed

#893 He
Rots
In
Love

#898 Her
Laugh
Haunts
Me

#894 That
Man
Almost
Raped me

#899 I love her
The rest
I lie to
Honest

#895 Almost
Counts
In
Everything

#900 My
Hero
Is
Burnt out

#901 Think
About
Every
Thing

#902 She
Felt
His
Pain

#903 She
Had
His
Baby

#904 She
Lived
His
Life

#905 Liar
You
Yes
You

#906 I never
Touched her
I still
Regret it

#907 When she
Calls
I feel
Invaded

#908 I
Pay
My
Friends

#909 Give
Birth
To
Reality

#910 Humans
As
Cannon
Fodder

#911 Loved
Her
To
Death

#912 Come
On
Let's
Fight

#913 I see her
I want her
I need her
Oh well

#914 She
Can
Not
Come

#915 Four
Consecutive
Life
Sentences

#916 Rape
Rape
Rape
Rape

#917 Nothing
Stands
Beyond
War

#918 I see
Women
As
Strangers

#919 His hand
Felt alien
On her
Breast

#920 Friends
In
The
Obituary

#921 She was
Cast out
She was
Happy

#926 He
Raped
Retarded
Men

#922 He cuts her
A line of coke
He takes her
Home

#927 Pigs
Drinking
Free
Coffee

#923 Money
Talks
You know
The rest

#928 She's ugly
She hates
To see
Her body

#924 Old woman
Head
In
Oven

#929 I sell
Myself
To avoid
Myself

#925 You can
Feel it
The air thick
Like blood

#930 Demons
Control
My
Eyes

#931 I look
Through
Women's
Clothes

#936 She was 20
Foul mouthed
Cruel
Pure beauty

#932 My tongue
Has
X-ray
Vision

#937 Beauty
Sunk its fangs
Into her flesh
And hung on

#933 Men clung
To her
Like
Drowning rats

#938 Relentless
Genius
Wore him
Away

#934 She
Touches me
My soul
Explodes

#939 60 hours
6 days
1 night
$3.25 per

#935 The night
Coughs blood
Breathes heavy
And waits

#940 It's
Kill
Yourself
Time

#941 Ugly
      No brains
      No tits
      No talent

#942 So many
      Beautiful women
      On the street
      Tonight

#943 She
      Showed me
      Her
      Tattoo

#944 Yes
      I am
      A
      Hater

#945 The world
      In my room
      In my head
      In my gun

#946 I will
      Kill
      Myself
      He said

#947 Two
      Faggots
      Checking
      Me

#948 He
      Likes
      To
      Suck

#949 Watery eyed
      Balding
      Pot bellied
      Queen

#950 Tonight
      The gun
      My mouth
      Oh yes

#951 Nothing
Can
Save
Her

#952 She shot
Her kids
And then
Herself

#953 Third abortion
She slashed
Her wrist
For god

#954 She uses
A smile
To hide
Her hate

#955 I hate
Men
But
You're different

#956 Beat
That
Jock's
Ass

#957 If you don't
Kill him
Then you don't
Come home

#958 Beat up
My boyfriend
I'll get
You stoned

#959 She shot
Herself
For my
Birthday present

#960 Father
Called
Me
Mister

#961 Black marine
Beating up
A fag
Georgetown

#962 She
Breaks
All
Hearts

#963 She
Is
Like
Winter

#964 He lost
His wife
He found
Happiness

#965 The abortion clinic
Nurses
Knew her
By name

#966 A baby
Born junky
Like mother
Like victim

#967 She found
Suicide
Her final
Resting place

#968 Insanity
Was a place
He checked into
And stayed

#969 Who
Has sex
With
Mongoloids

#970 Acquired
Immune
Deficiency
Syndrome

#971   Do you think
       She likes me?
       Do you?
       Do you?

#976   His father
       Taught abuse
       His son
       Learned truth

#972   Old woman
       Smoking and sleepy
       Died eyes closed
       Bed in flames

#977   Do
       Anything
       For
       Love

#973   No one
       Survives
       Her
       Lies

#978   Do
       Anything
       For
       Crack

#974   Her eyes
       Her perfume
       Her hair
       Ah summer

#979   A mass grave
       For
       The
       LAPD

#975   Lifetimes
       Living on streets
       Bums are
       Magicians

#980   She takes
       Photographs
       He takes
       Wallets

#981   She shoots
Pool
He shoots
Pigs

#982   She makes
Money
He makes
History

#983   She does
Work
He does
Time

#984   His beatings
Were brutal
He had
Steady customers

#985   I want
Too many
Women
So what

#986   They
Beat him up
At the
Public pool

#987   I
have
Grown
Insensitive

#988   She doesn't
Hate all kids
Just
Her's

#989   Identical twins
Sharing lovers
Sharing clothes
Sharing needles

#990   He
Kept
Hitting
Her

#991   We're
Dying
All
Dying

#992   He fell asleep
At the wheel
He destroyed
His family

#993   Fat drunk
Gun in mouth
Alone
Hot room

#994   A stuck pig
Bleeding sweat
This is it
Pull down

#995   Another
Drive
By
Shooting

#996   Smoking dust
Learning
To
Fly

#997   I tell
The lies
To all
The ladies

#998   This brutality
Is endless
This life
Is hell

#999   Home
From war
All dreams
Destroyed

#1000   Barrel in mouth
The moment!
The moment!
Goodbye